How to Influence People, Get Them to Like You, and Earn More Respect

52 Life-Changing Ideas for Self-Improvement. Improve Your Charisma, Communicate Better, Increase Your Status and Become an Effective Leader

A.V. Mendez

TABLE OF CONTENTS

Free Gift

As a thank you for getting this book, I would like to give you the initial report that you can use if you're not ready to commit to a long-term challenge just yet.

It's a short report called "The 10-Day Self-Improvement Challenge"

The goal of the report is not to replace this book. The goal of the report is to help you get started.

To help you fight that initial reluctance to take action, you can start small and start with a 10-day challenge instead.

You can download your copy by going to this link below:

https://mailchi.mp/85b284031873/45day

OTHER BOOKS

The 45-Day Self Improvement Handbook: 45 Daily Ideas, Habits and Action-Plan for Becoming More Productive, Persuasive, Influential, Sociable and Self- Confident

Build Confidence & Self-Esteem: 90 Awesome Techniques to Become Confident, Overcome Self-Doubt, Shyness and Improve Your Self-Esteem

How to Focus: 54 Habits, Tools and Ideas to Create Superhuman Focus, Eliminate Distractions, Stop Procrastination and Achieve More With Less Work

Stop Procrastination & Increase Productivity: 60 Tricks on How to Improve Your Focus, Time Management, Habits, Productivity and Overall Ability to Get Things Done

Improving Your Social & People Skills Guidebook: 77 Tricks on How to Improve Your Conversational Skills, Increase Self-Worth, and Become More Confident

Kindly search for "AV MENDEZ" on Amazon to checkout my other books.

Introduction

They always say that respect is earned, not given. It's not something that you just ask for. It's something that you gain through your status and value to the world.

The more valuable you are in the eyes of others and yourself, the more respect you'll gain. And the more respect you gain, the more influence and status you'll have.

So how do you become a person of value?

How do you attract respect without ever asking for it?

How do you build status without controlling other people's emotions… Without trying to be a bully…. Without inflicting fear on others…

You're not supposed to ask for respect. It's something that you get for being someone worth respecting.

If you want to gain other people's respect, then the answer is simply to be respectable. And to be respectable, there are small things that you can do and change in all aspects of your life.

In this short book, I am going to teach you 52 actionable ideas that you can implement ASAP.

These ideas are practical and something you can apply whoever you are. It doesn't matter what your job is. It doesn't matter how much money you make. It doesn't matter if you look like Brad Pitt or not.

The only thing that matters is your willingness to try the ideas inside the book.

So are you up for the challenge?

Are you willing to suspend your disbelief for a second and follow my advice?

Or are you "too full" of knowledge already that this lowly self-improvement book can't help you anymore?

If you are willing, then I'm sure that I can help you.

Part 1

Become a Person of Value

1 - Become a Person of Value

So what does becoming a person of value even mean?

It's actually pretty simple. To get respect from people, you have to be a value giver. That means sharing your knowledge to other people. Helping someone solve a problem. Creating a solution to make other people's misery disappear.

A person of value is someone who's constantly helping other people. The focus is not on your selfish desires. The focus is not on your own problems.

In fact, this is the main foundation of respect.

In life, you're either a value giver or a value taker.

If you are the former, then respect becomes automatic.

Action Guide:

1 - Ask yourself, how can I help someone today? It doesn't matter what the issue is. HELP SOMEONE ASIDE FROM YOURSELF.

2 - What problems can you help solve? This is where business ideas come from. Focus on what other people want and need and you'll have a business based on people's demand.

3 - When an opportunity arise, always choose to become a person of value instead of fading away in the background.

2 - Be the Best at What You Do

In order to become a person of value and gain respect, you have to never stop learning and be the best at what you do. Being the best at what you do lets you stand out from the crowd. People like someone who knows what he's doing. If you're the best mechanic, chef, writer, agent, etc. - then you automatically get respect from the people around you. You become this "mini-celebrity" in your market and respect becomes natural.

And to be the best at what you do, constant learning and practice are required. It usually takes between 5-7 years to become an "expert" at a certain skill. The more time and effort you put in, the better you become. The key is to LEARN and then ACT on what you learned.

Action Guide:

1 - Read a book about your topic. Start with the ones with lots of good reviews on Amazon. Then go deeper and start reading harder books about your main topic so you can learn more about it.

2 - Within 5 days after reading, apply at least 2 ideas from what you just learned.

3 - Take online courses from Udemy, Lynda, or Skillshare. Online courses are super cheap now and there's no reason not to take 2-3 online courses about your topic. Start with beginner classes then move up to more advanced ones once you implemented the lessons that you learned from the "beginner" classes.

3 - Respect Yourself

It's hard to get respect from other people if you don't even respect yourself.

Do you love yourself enough to actually take care of your body? Are you working on your insecurities? Are you giving yourself rewards for a job well done - in office and in your relationship?

Respecting yourself means knowing your own value. It's about knowing and acknowledging what you provide to the table.

If you know how to respect yourself, then other people will notice thus giving you this cycle of mutual respect.

Action Guide:

1 - Do stuff that reinforces your belief that you respect yourself. Go to the gym, have a morning ritual, go for a run every day, take care of your body and watch what you eat.

2 - Treat yourself every once in a while. Have a cheat day, go on awesome vacations, get a massage every 2 weeks - anything that shows that you respect yourself is good!

3 - Take care of your personal hygiene. Make sure that you're always brushing your teeth, using a deodorant, using great shampoo, washing your face, and take good care of your sensitive areas. Good personal hygiene shows that you actually care about yourself.

4 - Respect Other People

Sometimes, respect is a 2-way street. Although you might respect other people who you don't know personally, deeper and real respect comes from having a 2-way relationship. If you know how to respect a person, then it will show and they might give you the same respect that you have for them. The cliche says that "Respect begets respect."

And I 100% agree with that. Treating people the right way usually leads to others making more effort to please you and making sure that you feel good about yourself.

Action Guide:

1 - Before you demand respect, make sure that you respect yourself first.

2 - Before you demand respect, make sure that you respect OTHER people first.

3 - Make other people feel good about themselves. Stroke their ego if you have to (although you should be aware when other people do this to you). Praise them, mention their accomplishments especially when other people hear it. The more you do this, the more they'll like you and the more respect you will get.

4 - Before you meet people who are big on your market, research some of their accomplishments first so you'll know exactly the praise that you can give them when you finally meet each other in person.

5 - Be Humble

Nobody likes a bragger.

Instead of bragging about your accomplishments, focus on giving praise to other people. Focus on what others did that is cool, awesome and helpful.

Being humble means not thinking about what other people would think of you when you did a certain deed.

Being humble means knowing when to shut up and when to speak.

Being humble means knowing when you can be valuable and knowing when to just listen to others.

Being humble means knowing when you made a mistake, and owning to that mistake like a real man or woman.

Action Guide:

1 - Never brag about your accomplishments. Nobody really cares about it.

2 - Self-deprecation is good (to a point). When others praise you, say thank you but always give credit to other people as well.

3 - Don't let your ego get too big that you can't control it anymore. Others may use it against you and control your feelings just by stroking your ego and making you feel good about yourself (which is great but only if it's natural).

6 - Be Genuinely Interested in What Others Have to Say

Do you zone out every time someone talks to you? Do you think about your response even before somebody finishes talking?

Then you are a passive listener.

You only care about what you have to say… and you only care about your own response.

In order to gain respect, you have to understand other people on a deeper level. One of the ways to do that is to listen with intent. Be genuinely interested in what they have to say. Don't think about a witty or funny response.

What you can do instead is to ask interesting questions related to what she is talking about.

If she's talking about how her dog dies, don't tell her about your neighbor's dog. Instead, ask questions like:

What's her name?
How long have you been with her?
What's her breed?

These are questions that will make them talk. Your job is to listen 70% of the time. The less you speak, and the more your conversation partner does, the better.

Action Guide:

1 - Listen with intent. Make sure that you really understand what they are talking about.

2 - Ask good questions. Good questions are the ones that will make them talk more about the topic. Good questions make others think and ponder. The better your questions are, the better your conversation will be. And people trust people who know how to listen and ask the right questions.
3 - People can feel when you're genuine and when you're just floating around your own universe. Practice listening with intent in your next conversation. Do not think about any response that is about you. The focus should be about what your conversation partner is talking about.

7 - Understand the Other Party's Perspective

People respect other people who understand them.

Have you ever met a person and you felt like "he just gets it?."

That's the power of empathy. The power to relate to what the other person is feeling.

Empathy allows you to put yourself in their position and understand why they act the way they act. It lets you stop judging and forces you to start understanding.

Action Guide:

1 - Practice empathy. What does this other person feel right now? Sadness? Happiness? Regret? Know the feeling so you can relate more to the other person.

2 - Be the person they can talk to whenever they need a confidant. Someone who would listen and someone who wouldn't judge. If you can get them to open up with you, then that means they trust you and they respect you. Do not break that trust and never ever make that conversation between the both of you.

8 - Start a Podcast

The next 4 ideas are about building a "celebrity" like status in your own market/industry.

Being a celebrity doesn't necessarily mean that everybody knows you. It's about having a slice of the population in your industry who likes and respect you.

If you're a celebrity in your niche, then respect becomes almost automatic. A celebrity gets the status whether you like it or not.

So how do we manufacture celebrity?

We do it by being an expert in what we do and showing other people that, yes, we are indeed an expert.

Through a podcast, a book, and Facebook value posts - we can manufacture a celebrity like status in the eyes of our followers (market/industry).

Let's start with a Podcast.

A podcast allows you to show your expertise in your topic. The more you talk about your topic, the more trust you'll gain from your listeners.

In addition, you can also invite other experts and be the interviewer. Doing this builds your legend through association. If you invite awesome people on your show, then you will be associated with them through your podcast - this giving you a boost in your market's celebrity status.

Action Guide:

1 - Think of a topic that you want to talk about.

2 - Choose a format. Do you want it to be a solo podcast? Or do you want to interview other people? Both works but I recommend the latter if you're just starting out and nobody knows you yet.

3 - Start with cheap equipment if you have to. There's no need to buy a $500 mic and every fancy editing software out there.

4 - Choose a podcast site host like podbean.com or soundcloud.com

9 - Write and Publish a Book

Nothing beats "EXPERT STATUS/CELEBRITY MAKER STATUS" more, than a good olé book.

A book has a high value and the majority of people think that only experts can write a book.

If you have a book on your topic, you are automatically seen as an expert in your field.

You get invited to speaking gigs. You get to builds fans who like and respect you because you've given them something of value through your book.

Having a book is a new calling card. Instead of giving away cards, start giving away books on networking events so you'll standout and gain instant respect from other people.

Action Guide:

1 - Choose a topic that you want to write about.

2 - I recommend getting these books on Amazon:

The 90 Minute Book Outline
The Self-Published Entrepreneur
On Writing Well

How to Write a Non-Fiction (Joanna Penn)

3 - Start outlining and start writing your book!

10 - Facebook Value Posts

FB Value Posts are usually slightly longer posts about your topic. It's about giving insights about different sub-topics under your main one.

Let's say that you're an expert when it comes to dating women. In one of your posts, you can talk about how to approach women. In another post, you can talk about how to have the right mindset so you can approach women.

Basically, a FB value post gives you an "expert like status" since you are giving some kind of new information or perspective about a certain topic.

In addition, getting likes and comments helps other people see your posts. Now, don't get caught up with likes and comments in the beginning.

Just focus on creating value for other people. Keep posting great information/stories on your wall and be generous in giving them what they want and need.

Action Guide:

1 - Brainstorm some topics you can write about.

2 - Follow other people on your niche and look at what they are doing when it comes to their FB value posts.

3 - Write at least 2 new value posts every week. Comment back in every single comment on your posts if possible.

4 - Make them ponder about your post. Always ask a question at the end of every post and encourage them to post their answer in the comment section.

5 - Ask them questions and be genuinely interested in their response (please see idea #6 *Be Genuinely Interested in What Others Have to Say).*

11 - YouTube Vlogging

Another one that builds an almost instant celebrity status is vlogging.

Creating a vlog allows you to share your thoughts and even your life in just 5-10 minutes of video.

It also allows you to share your expertise. A lot of online coaches nowadays are sharing their expertise via short 5-15 minute videos about sub-topics under their main expertise.

These videos build value, trust and a celebrity like following that gain you instant respect. When people see that you're giving value to the world, then you automatically get the respect that you deserve.

Action Guide:

1 - Choose a topic that you want to vlog about.

2 - Go to YouTube and see what topics your competitors are talking about in their videos.

3 - Start today. You don’t need a fancy camera to get started. Use your smartphone and just hit record.

4 - Focus on creating quality content and be consistent with your uploads. For beginners, in order to gain traction, you need to post at least 2-3 videos a week.

12 - Dress Appropriately

Although we are in an era where you cannot just judge people based on what they wear, how other people dress still dictates how we look at them, especially if it's the first time we're meeting them.

The truth is, people judge a book by its cover. And it's the same with what we wear. If you look like a homeless person, then there's no way you can get a million dollar deal. You need to wear something respectable. Something with more appeal than your shorts and your flip flops.

Is it unfair to judge someone based on what he wears? Probably. But that doesn't change the reality that how you dress affects how we think about you.

You don't need to spend thousands of dollars to dress well. However, you do need to invest some money especially when you're just starting out to build your wardrobe.

In addition, dressing well means dressing according to the occasion or event (and weather). Where are you going? What is the weather today? Do you really need to wear a 3 piece suit or a suit and tie would do?

Action Guide:

1 - Match your dress with the occasion or location you are going to. With formal events, you can never go wrong with a nice fitting suit and tie. For women, a simple dress would do.

2 - Always remember this. The FIT MAKES THE DRESS. You can have the most expensive cloth but if it does not fit well, then it still wouldn't look respectable. Spend money on a nice fitting suit or dress and you would easily look like a million dollar man or woman.

3 - Overdressing is better than underdressing.

4 - Smile whenever you meet other people. Your smile is a part of your whole attire.

Part 2
Know How to Act Well

13 -Stop Being Too Nice

Being too nice gets you abused.

People start thinking that they can ask you anything and you would always say yes.

Being too nice gets you taken advantage of.

Instead of being too nice, know when to be nice and know when to taper off.

Nice people think that people will like them just because they are nice. No. It doesn't work that way. Instead of being nice, be likable instead. A likable person is someone who makes other people comfortable around them, knows his value, and understands other people on a deeper level.

Action Guide:

1 - Be aware and know when you're already getting abused for how nice you are.

2 - Don't expect other people to like you and even love you just because you're a nice person. The game is still about VALUE. Are you adding some kind of value to their life? If Yes, then respect gets easier.

3 - Practice saying NO to other people's requests.

14 - Choose Your Battles Well

Just because something will give you recognition doesn't mean you should go for it.

You have to be humble enough to know when you are and when you aren't ready for something.

Choose your battles well. You do not go into a war with a chopstick. You need guns, ammo, armor, shield, etc.

You gain respect by giving a good fight. If you're just going to get mauled, then you're only going to get mockery.

In order to gain respect, you have to stand toe to toe with an enemy. You have to be able to give something worth watching. Whatever field you are in, make sure that you choose your battles well. Choose something where there's a reasonable chance of success.

Action Guide:

1 - Know when something is still worth pursuing or not. Do not feed your ego by keep on going through something because you'll gain respect when you achieve it. Some battles just aren't worth pursuing.

15 - Apologize for Your Mistakes

A lot of us are afraid to apologize because of our ego. We think that apologizing means we're taking 100% of the blame. We think that if we apologize, that means we're the "smaller" person and we're the one who's the main reason why everything gets messed up.

However, when you are genuine and when you know you made some mistakes, apologizing tends to gain respect from other people.

When you apologize, that means you *man, up* and you accept the consequences of your action.

That shows bravery, humility, honesty, and accountability. Qualities that gains respect faster than anything.

Action Guide:

1 - If you made a mistake, then be the first one to apologize. Apologizing is a sign of strength and character. You are not losing your dignity or pride by admitting a mistake that you did.

2 - Always ask yourself the lessons that you learned from a specific mistake. Take down some notes and make sure that you remember it so you won't get to do it again.

3 - Always vow to yourself and to the other person that you will improve. This mindset shifts it what separates someone who is not worth respecting to someone worth respecting.

16 - Do Not Gossip

As humans, we are natural gossipers. It's human nature to always keep talking- to keep sharing, to share secrets.

However, as natural as it is, sometimes, we have to fight the urge to gossip.

The irony about gossiping is we like gossiping but we hate people who gossip. That doesn't make sense but it is what it is.

People who gossip do not gain any respect from people who have a higher value than them. High-value creators are attracted to people who are honest, and people who have integrity.

Action Guide:

1 - Fight the urge to talk about people. Instead, start talking about ideas that can bring value to other people.

2 - Never say anything bad against someone in public that you wouldn't say to that person in person.

3 - Practice the art of stopping people from gossiping. Whenever you notice that your group goes deeper and deeper into talking about someone, the more you should be wary of the situation and know when to stop the conversation.

17 - Know the Difference Between Confident and Arrogant

There's a fine line between confidence and arrogance. The choice is clear. You never want to be arrogant but you always need to be confident.

Confidence is the belief in yourself backed up by results and your own skills, work-ethic and potential.

Arrogance is the belief in yourself without the results. It's something that comes out of nowhere. Arrogance is also the lack of humility to accept that you're not as good as you thought you are.

Focus on building self-confidence but make sure that you don't cross the line. Be confident but be humble. Do not brag, and do not shame. In short, do not be a total a$$hole.

Action Guide:

1 - Always know the difference between confidence and arrogance.

2 - Notice whenever you feel the need to brag. Notice whenever you feel superior to someone. Control this feeling and get yourself back to the ground. You don't need to brag for you to get noticed. If you're good at what you do, then you will get noticed.

3 - Read books about self-confidence. Shameless plug, you can start with my book "Maximum Confidence."

18 - Kill Your Ego

People will argue that Kanye West is successful and he has a Texas-size ego. And that's true, he does have a Texas-size ego and he is successful. But the thing about Kanye is he's so talented and creative that he's still successful IN SPITE of his ego. I would imagine that he'll be even more successful and more respected if not for his ego.

His ego actually makes him vulnerable. His ego is his enemy. He could've been the greatest rapper/creative of all time. But his ego is so big that it's hindering his full potential.

Also, do you even respect Kanye? Half the people loathe him. Do you love his music? Probably. Do you like Kanye? I have my reservations.

It's the same with us all. It doesn't matter what your job or profession is. Kill the ego and you'll be more successful, happy, fulfilled, and respected.

Action Guide:

1 - Always remember that ego is never a good thing. There are no positive side effects of being egoistic. Confidence, you should have. Ego? Never.

2 - Be aware of your own feelings. Stop the ego before it begins to eat your whole character. Never let it define who you are as a person. People who has big egos can become successful, but they will always be less respected.

19 - Be Proactive

Have you ever had an employee who always needs supervision in every little thing that he does? How does that work out for you? Probably ain't good eh?

Whatever your profession is, you always want to deal with proactive people.

People who make an effort. People who take the lead. People who know the value of action.

Proactive people are the ones who will set the tone for the meeting. Proactive people are the ones who will do the research even before you asked them to. Proactive people are the ones who will make plans and follow them.

The more proactive a person is, the more respect he gets. We like proactive people because we like getting lead. We like people who knows how to take control.

Even if yours isn't particularly a position of power, you can still do a lot of things that other people will notice.

You just have to learn how to take charge and lead.

Action Guide:

1 - Be proactive in everything that you do. If you want something to be done, then start it yourself.

2 - Hire people who know the value of being a leader.

20 - Do What You Say You Would Do

This is pretty simple. We hate people who never walk the talk. We don't like people who always promise the world but never really do something about it. We dislike people who say something and does another.

If you want to be respected, then you have to be true to your words.

In fact, this is one of the most important codes of any organization. Heck, even evil organizations know the importance of their words. For them, their word is their bond.

Simply put, if you say something, then you have to do it.

Trust takes years to build but one lie and one mishap would make it crumble into dust.

Action Guide:

1 - Always follow up on something you say you would do.

2 - Remember that you instantly lose trust and status the moment you broke a promise or not do something you said you would do.

3 - I recommend that you read the report Honor Among Thieves.

Here's the link:

https://philarchive.org/archive/SANHAT-8v1

21 - Always Be On Time

My God. I hate late people.

Late people always seem to have a reason why they're late. It's damn annoying. And it's so damn disrespectful.

Being late shows that you do not value the other person's time.

Being late means you do not value your own time.

If you're a chronically late person, then you have to accept the fact that something has to change. If not, then you will stay disrespectful or someone who people do not trust.

Action Guide:

1 - Know the reasons why you are always late. Identify the main root of the problem. And no, it's not the external stuff like traffic or the location of your house. Most likely, these are things like: the time you sleep, the time you wake up, how long you spend in the shower, etc.

2 - Next, set a timer for every task that you need to do. Make sure that you have ample amount of time for each task.

3 - Create the habit of having a set amount of time for each task. If you shower for 15 minutes in the morning, then make sure that you don't get past that time frame. Or else, the other tasks schedule will get messed up.

22 - Start Leading

Of all the people we associate ourselves with, who are the ones we like, trust, and respect?

Most likely, they are the ones who know how to lead properly.

Jack Ma said people don't leave jobs. They leave horrible bosses.

Whether you're the manager or the staff, make sure that you know how to lead other people.

Be so good in your job that they can't ignore you.

Focus on creating results that other people will naturally notice. Trust me, if you know how to bring in the results, then other people's admiration becomes automatic.

Action Guide:

1 - Start leading by being proactive in your daily tasks.

2 - Focus on doing your job well, not on trying to impress other people. Just do what you are supposed to do and respect will come naturally.

3 - I recommend reading books like:

The Dichotomy of Leadership & Extreme Ownership by *Jocko Willink*

23 - Point Out Other People's Mistakes in Private

If you are a leader, then you will eventually find people's mistakes over and over again.

You can berate them in public and tell them how stupid they are, or you can talk to them in private and help them realize their mistake/s.

It sounds to me that the latter would be more beneficial for the whole organization.

I have a bad temper, and sometimes, I say and do things that I wished I haven't done. This created a bad image for me and I've been paying the price ever since. Hopefully, you'll learn from my mistake and try to "hold off your horses"

Be patient and learn to do constructive criticisms in private.

Action Guide:

1 - Never berate or lecture anyone in public.

2 - Talk to someone in private so you guys can fix the mistake.

3 - Provide constructive criticism and let the other person know that you just want the best for her and the organization.

24 - Stand for What You Believe is to Be True

Why do people still respect people who are known criminals?

Why does are society like to glorify bad people?

Why do we like to put people on a pedestal?

It's because we like people who stand for something. We like people who believe in something - whatever that is.

Obviously, this can get out of control like Hitler did.

But I would assume you're no Hitler and you want the best for other people.

So what can you offer the world that other people cannot? Try to come up with that something.

If you do this, you will get recognition, admiration, and respect from other people. By focusing on the mission, you'll be able to change lives of hundreds, thousands or even millions of people.

Action Guide:

1 - Stand for what you believe is true. If that thing can help other people, then that's even better.

2 - You have to be the first one to believe in your idea. If not, then other people will notice and your idea will just turn into dust.

25 - Take Care of Your Family

In the TV series Game of Thrones, Brienne of Tarth has this amazing quote that says "Nothing is more hateful than failing to protect the one you love."

And for the most of us, that'll be our family.

It doesn't necessarily have to be blood relative. Your friends, cousins and everyone you love is considered family.

And when I say "protect" your family, I mean that in the literal sense of the word.

Protect them physically. Don't let others bully and hurt them.

Make sure that they are safe and sound. Make sure that they have the capability to protect themselves in case of danger.

Action Guide:

1 - Protect your family physically. Make sure that they are safe anywhere they go. You can do this by:

- Making sure that your house is safe from intruders
- Letting your family attend self-defense classes
- Attending BJJ classes
- Learning how to shoot a gun

2 - Bonus: Get insurance so your family doesn't have to suffer financially in case of your sudden death.

Part 3
Service and the Art of Connecting

26 - Solve Other People's Problems

Do you want to get rich? Do you want other people's admiration? Do you want to get other people's respect even without demanding for it?

Then you have to become a problem solver.

A problem solver is someone who focuses on other people.

Instead of focusing on how much money you can make, focus on the problems that you can solve.

What are the desires, wants, and needs of other people that you can solve for them?

Become a problem solver and you'll attract other people naturally.

Action Guide:

1 - Always be aware of the possible opportunities to help other people.

2 - Actively find and solve other people's problems. The most respected people on Earth are the ones who have solved big problems for us. And it doesn't even have to be a problem per se, it could be a want or a desire that someone needs to be fulfilled. Like the desire for entertainment and the likes.

27 - Stand Up for Someone Else

Bravery.

It's one of the most adored and wanted value, especially in America. We honor our soldiers with dignity and respect - and deservedly so. They literally put their life on the line of duty. They are here to serve and protect.

Now, you don't have to be in the military to stand for someone else. You can be a protector even if you're just a normal civilian.

The most important thing here is to be on the side of the good.

When you see someone being disrespected, stand up and protect the other person.

When you see someone getting bullied, stand up and fight for what is right.

When you see racism around you, stand up for what is moral.

Action Guide:

1 - Always choose to stand up for someone else, especially if you know that it is right and just. Don't think about what other people would think. Don't worry about the praise or criticism you'll receive. If you know and believe that something is right, then you have to stand for it.

28 - Acknowledge Someone's Opinion

Nobody likes being told that he is wrong.

We don't want the humiliation of being wrong, especially in public.

If you don't agree to a certain person's belief on something, then you don't have to pretend and say that you do.

However, what you need to do is acknowledge their own beliefs.

Just by acknowledging other people, you'll easily avoid awkward conversations. You'll also avoid heated arguments that never turn into something productive.

Action Guide:

1 - Acknowledge someone's point of view and never blatantly tell them that they are wrong. You're never going to have a productive discussion if you do this.

What you can do instead is to say something like:

"I see that you don't mind abortion after 6 months, and I do get where you're coming from. You believe that it's the mother's choice. I do think that we also have to consider the baby's life…."

Don't use the word BECAUSE or BUT unless necessary. I like to just follow it up with my own take. You can also use the words "and" and "also" if you want to.

29 - Calm Your Nerves

Who would you rather take the last shot? Michael Jordan or some random nervous NBA player? Obviously, it's Michael Jordan.

Why? Because he has the ability to calm his nerves even in clutch and close-game situations.

It's the same with whatever your profession is. You have to be calm and set as an example to your staff. You have to learn how to take control of situations. You have to be the face of the company during stressful situations.

By doing this, people will follow your example and you will serve as the inspiration for them to do the same thing.

Action Guide:

1 - Watch your initial reactions to stressful situations and deadlines? Are you freaking out and acting irrationally? Or are you taking control and being a leader?

2 - Be aware and then change your initial reaction. Focus on calming your nerves and then make sure that other people (your staff, friends, boss) do the same.

30 - Do Not Miss a Deadline!

Do you trust people who always misses a deadline?

Do you like working with them?

Do you even respect them?

The answers are no, no and no.

We like and respect people who are competent at what they do. We like people who are always beating deadlines and submitting quality work.

It doesn't matter if you're the boss or the staff. We all have some kind of deadline to beat and we should do all we can to do so.

The more deadlines you beat, the more people will respect you for what you can bring to the table.

Action Guide:

1 - Learn to prioritize your tasks. Know what is urgent, important and *important & urgent.*

2 - Always tell the other person in advance if you think that the deadline is an impossible feat to beat. Be honest now so you don't have to suffer later.

3 - Never miss a deadline. I mean, you know what happens when you do.

31 - Associate Yourself with Respectable People

This one has an instant effect.

Just by simply hanging out with respectable people, you instantly get to associate yourself with them.

That means if one group of people is revered for their generosity, then you instantly become generous yourself - at least in the eyes of other people outside that group.

Now, association by the group also has a negative effect.

If you hang out with addicts, then there's a good chance that you'll turn into an addict as well.

So use this carefully and make sure that you hangout with the right people.

Action Guide:

1 - Make new friends. Friends who are good for you. Friends who will support you all the way.

2 - Hangout with people you like to become. Do you want to be good with Math? Weird, but okay - hangout with mathematicians. DUH. Do you want to be a great entrepreneur, join business masterminds and learn from other entrepreneurs on your field.

3 - Stop hanging out with your current friends, or at least, lessen the time you spend with them if your goals and interest doesn't match anymore.

32 - Be a Connector

A connector is someone who introduces other people to each other.

From strangers to partners. From strangers to friends.

That's what you want to happen to people you introduce to each other. The value of the connector is in his status. Connectors are the one who binds the 2 people/groups together. Be a connector and you'll never have to worry about referrals ever again.

Be a connector and trust, respect, and gratitude with always be there.

Action Guide:

1 - Start hosting dinners for other entrepreneurs (actors, players, whatever your profession is).

2 - Introduce people to each other and be the main connector of the group. By doing this, you'll have a high status in their perspective, and this can lead to more business deals in the future.

3 - Try to limit dinners for 15-30 people at a time. Too many guests and it'll get expensive fast. Also, it'll be harder to manage a large group so start with at least 5-10. Then expand up to 30 maximum.

33 - Do Not Forget People's Name

Unless you're a Starbucks Barista, then botching other people's name is a surefire way to lose trust and likeability from the other person's perspective.

Remembering names is a sign of respect and admiration.

It's the best sound that we'll ever want to hear.

Our name will always be something unique to us (even if you have someone who has the same name as you do). Most of the time, spelling and surnames will differ anyway.

Action Guide:

1 - Build the habit of creating your list of important people that you can do business with in the future.

2 - Write any important things you know about the person on a piece of a small index card. Put their name, contact number, interests, and any other details that may help you remember them.

3 - Use this index card and read it before you meet the person again. You can also review these cards every once in a while so you can be ready just in case you meet them randomly.

34 - Find Something Unique About the Person and Take Note of It

One of the fastest ways to get other people's trust is to complement them. Complement their hair, their clothes, their style, their car, whatever…

Complement them however big or small that thing is.

The key here is to just focus on one good small quality that they might have.

Action Guide:

1 - Find something unique about other people.

2 - Notice this one thing and make sure that they're not insecure about it. Complement whatever that is and stroke other people's ego if you must. Now, you should be genuine in your complements and not just do it because you want to get their trust.

3 - Find something new. Maybe new shoes, new hairstyle, new laptop, new anything. If it's new, then they would want other people to notice it.

4 - Don't ever act fake around them. People notice if you're genuine or just doing it for show.

35 - Do Act of Random Coolness

You know what's cool and respectable?

Someone who's kind and always do an act of random coolness.

Yeah, it's basically just about being a decent person.

It's about the small things.

Opening the door for someone. Waiting for someone in the elevator. Helping an old lady cross the street. Picking up some random litter.

Do these small things and you'll become someone worth respecting and admiring.

Action Guide:

1 - Do at least 2 act of random kindness today. At first, it will be a little bit forced. But once you get the habit of doing something for other people, this will be easier and effortless. Basically, you'll be someone genuinely worth admiring and respecting - but that's only if you do it with the best intentions.

36 - Respect Other People's Time

If you don't know how to respect other people's time, then how can you expect them to respect yours?

Respect is a two-way street and it's something you have to work on - forever. It's given, and it can also be taken away in a snap! You make the wrong move and your reputation turns to shambles.

One of the reputation killers is always being late and always changing the time of a meet-up or a meeting.

Being late all the time shows to the other person that "I do not value your time and what you put in the table." It shows that "I'm better than you, I'm the alpha so you should be the one waiting, instead of the other way around."

If you have this mindset, then people will go behind you and stab you in the back. Nobody likes a smug, more specifically a "time smug."

Action Guide:

1 - Practice the habit of being on time. Always make it a goal to be there at least 5 minutes before your expected time of arrival.

2 - If you're always late, then stop blaming other people or circumstances. Take ownership of your own results and never blame it on others.

37 - Do Not Leave the Office Too Early

I used to be the one who's always first out the door.

I thought I would even be rewarded for this because I always finished my tasks ahead of time.

Basically, while everyone is still chatting, rumbling or working, I was already munching on my bread and on the way out of the office. I was productive and I was proud of it.

But I never get any recognition for it.

In fact, my boss even took an issue because I was always the first one to leave. He thought that my tasks are super easy and he added at least 50% on my work load. F*CK.

Learn to adapt, especially if you are an employee. I'm not saying you shouldn't try to be productive. However, you should also show your commitment to the company by not being the first one out the door every day.

Action Guide:

1 - Never be the one to leave the office first. If everybody leaves at 5 pm, have a little leeway and leave at around 5:10 pm instead.

2 - Show others that you're actually putting in the work. Unfortunately, it's not just about your results. It's also about how much time and effort you put in every single day. Let other people see you as a hard worker.

38 - Raise Your Standards

Standards are set for a reason. If we don't have standards, then we won't be friends with the right people, have the best employees, have the best business, etc.

Your standard is what set you apart from other people.

Having high standards means you'll also attract people who also have the same mindset as you.

By doing this, you'll be able to connect with the right people - find the right buyers, attract investors, and get repeat customers.

Increase your standard and your expectations for yourself and you'll also increase your results.

And when you're great at what you do, you also attract natural respect from other respectable people.

Action Guide:

1 - Always set a standard for all the tasks that you do. Make sure that your standard is better than most people would expect so you can overdeliver.

2 - Never overpromise and underdeliver. Do the slight opposite instead. OVERPROMISE BUT ALSO, OVERDELIVER.

3 - Focus on providing value to other people. It's better to get paid less for more results than to let your customers feel underwhelmed by the results of what you're selling.

39 - Talk Less, Listen More

I used to talk a lot. I want to be right. I want to be heard. I want to be the center of attention. But I soon realized that this doesn't serve me well. It just made other people hate me.

Instead of talking more, the secret to gaining other people's trust is to talk less and listen more.

Focus on what the other person has to say and make a reply based on what they say, not on what you want to share.

If you do this one thing, you'll be able to gain respect than any other people you know. You don't need to be rich and well connected to listen. You just need an open mind and the ability to focus on the other person.

Action Guide:

1 - Focus on what the other person has to say. Don't share your story or what happened to you. Instead, reply with assurance, empathy, sympathy, and understanding.

Ex.

If your friend is broker hearted, don't talk about the time when you got broken hearted. Instead, tell the other person that "I can't imagine the pain that you're feeling right now. But I am here to listen" - or something like that. Got it?

2 - Talk 20% of the time and listen 80% of the time.

40 - Become an A+ Public Speaker

Do you want to learn how to command an audience?

Do you want to have the instinct of someone who knows how to turn bad experiences into good ones?

Do you want people to see you as someone inspirational and aspirational?

Then you have to learn how to become a good public speaker.

A good public speaker is someone who knows how to take control of the audience's attention. The more attention they put into you, the more you become someone they admire and like to become. This brings in more respect and more admiration, even more so, it's something natural and not forced.

Action Guide:

1 - Commit to becoming a good public speaker.

2 - Attend Toastmasters meetings in your area.

3 - Start small. First, talk to 3 people, then 10, then 15, and so on. Focus on improving every single talk.

4 - Understand that it's okay to mess up at the time. I recommended that you start small so you don't have to put yourself in an uncomfortable situation since you're just a beginner right now.

41 - Stand Up Straight

Aside from the negative physical effects of hunching, not standing up straight also shows insecurity, vulnerability, weakness, and other negative connotations.

When we see someone who stands up straight, we automatically see someone confident. Someone who's worth respecting.

Is it unfair and somehow weird that that's the case? It is.

But I don't even try to question why we think that way.

All I know is standing up straight shows confidence.

It shows that you are a leader who knows how to take command and someone others can look up to.

Action Guide:

1 - Awareness is the key. Always be aware of your own posture. Stand up straight or sit up straight. It gives others a better impression of you, plus it also helps in making you healthier and lets you avoid back pain in the long-term.

42 - The 60/40 Eye Contact Rule

Observing eye contact has been one of the best ways to know whether someone is listening to you or not. It's also a great indicator of a person's comfortability level around you.

The better you are with eye contact, the more likely you are to be perceived as someone trustworthy.

What I recommend is you follow the 60/40 eye contact rule.

Basically, you look at the person in the eye 60% of the time. Try to look at the person's eye whenever he's telling something really important. Also, I often do eye contact at the beginning of each sentence and then I include a slight nod to show that I am listening.

This works pretty well for me as it is the right blend of eye contact and no eye-contact.

Action Guide:

1 - Follow the 60/40 eye contact rule. Look when your conversation partner is saying something important.

2 - When you're the one speaking, look in the eye of your conversation partner when you're trying to say or imply something important.

Part 4
Self-Improvement Strategies

43 - Use a Wide Range of Voice Tonality

You can't be monotone and expect people to not think that you're some kind of weirdo.

You need to use a wide range of voice tonality that shows the emotion behind your words.

When you know how to use a wide range of voice tonality, you are less likely to be misunderstood. You are less likely to be thought of as angry when you aren't, or sad when you're really happy.

Show your emotion through your tone and other people will understand you much better - emotionally and practically speaking.

Action Guide:

1 - Practice in front of the mirror. Practice speaking in a wide range of emotion/state like: angry, sad, disappointed, sarcasm, happy, ecstatic, excited, etc.

This may seem silly to do but it can help you when you apply it in real life.

2 - Warning: Know how to use sarcasm well because one misunderstood sarcasm can make other people hate you.

44 - Speak Clearly - Do Not Speak Too Fast, Talk Slower - Speak in Low Volume

Alright, that is a mouthful, so let's get to it one by one.

Speak Clearly

Sometimes, we don't notice it but we tend to speak in a manner that some people cannot understand. Speaking clearly means having the right tone and right pronunciation of the words.

Do Not Speak Too Fast, Talk Slower

Speaking too fast can make other people misunderstand what you're saying. Speak on a slightly slower pace than usual. This can also help you speak clearly because you're talking at a slower pace.

Speak in Low Volume

You do not need to speak louder in order to get heard. In fact, you should try lowering your voice so you can see how others react.

Action Guide:

1 - Practice speaking clearly in front of the mirror. I recommend reading a short poem over and over again.

2 - Stop talking too fast! Most people won't understand what you have to say.

3 - If you're in a small room and you want other people to listen to what you have to say, speak in a lower volume and let them come closer to you.

45 - Do Not Complain on Public

I bet that you have friends in real life, on Facebook, or in work that never seem to run out of things to complain about.

Do you see them as someone to look up to? Do you have more respect for them because of it? Nahhhhh. You don't.

Although we like complaining ourselves, we really hate to see and hear other people complain.

There's just too much negativity out there and a friend adding drama to your life is just not worth it.

Don't be a public complainer. People will start to see you as someone with low status. Someone who cannot control their emotions. Someone weak and someone they cannot trust to lead.

Action Guide:

1 - Watch what you have to say before you blurt it out on the public. It may be something that you'll regret saying. So watch your words carefully so you don't mess things up.

2 - If you have to complain about someone or something, make it a private affair. You should only complain to the responsible parties.

3 - Do not complain or post your personal problems on social media. Nobody gives a f*ck anyway. If you need professional guidance, then go to a doctor/psychologist/therapist to talk to.

46 - Seek Out Constructive Criticism

The most respectable people are the ones who know and understand that they won't be perfect in everything they do.

They know that they will make mistakes just like everybody else. That's why they constantly seek out constructive criticism from other people below and above him.

Constructive criticism is a criticism that is sincere and has value. A criticism that has a suggestion on how to turn the situation around.

Action Guide:

1 - Forget about your ego and accept criticism from other people.

2 - Know who cares about you and know who hates you. The best constructive criticisms are the ones based on tough love. Some criticisms are just based on them hating on you.

3 - Always ask the other person what you can do to make the situation better. What are the action steps that you need to take in order to make things right?

47 - Study Influence and Persuasion

As I've told you already, being a leader gets you respected. And a leader is someone who knows how to manage situations.

One of the most important skills you should learn is Influence and Persuasion.

Influence and Persuasion aren't about manipulating other people. It's about showing them a better path that will lead them to achieve their own desires.

So don't use persuasion for evil. Other people will suffer, and karma will get back to you sooner than later.

In order to influence people, you need to know what they desire. What are the things that they want to achieve? Give them a path to take and they will follow you as long as you show them the results that they want to get.

Action Guide:

1 - Start reading books about persuasion and influence. Here are the best ones to start with:

48 Laws of Power by Robert Greene
Influence by Robert Cialdini
How to Win Friends and Influence People by Dale Carnegie

2 - Study Copywriting (salesmanship in print)

Read books like:

The Adweek Copywriting Handbook by *Joe Sugarman*

Cashvertising by *Eric Drew Whitman*

Breakthrough Advertising by *Eugene Schwartz*

3 - Start selling something. Sell anything on a garage sale, eBay, Amazon, or craigslist. You'll only be able to improve your persuasion and influence skills through practice.

48 - Ask Life-Changing Questions

They say that the quality of your life will depend on the quality of questions you ask yourself.

People who ask the right questions usually get the right answer. They are the one who "make it" in life.

They are the ones who are doing something good about what they are given.

Strive to be this kind of person. Someone others look up to not because of his wealth but because of the way he lives his life.

Action Guide:

A - Ask questions that can't be answered by a yes or a no.

B - Ask questions like:

Note: Only ask these questions to people you already have a relationship with. A mere colleague would find these a little weird. However, you can ask these to yourself as well.

1 - If you become like the 3 people you hang around with the most, who would you become?

2 - Where will you be in 3 years if you keep going in this direction?

3 - What would do if you were the only one judging yourself?

4 - What would you do, if you couldn't fail?

5 - Who do you love? What are you doing about it?

6 - When is the last time you celebrated?

7 - If no one knew how old you were, how old would you be?

8 - If all the people you helped today helped you, how much help would you receive?

9 - What are you grateful for? (I think this is an excellent question to ask at the end of every day – by the way, research shows that writing down what you're grateful for daily will make you happier.)

Source: https://www.bradaronson.com/questions-to-ask/

49 - Don't Be Afraid to Believe in Something

There will always be 2 sides of the coin. There will be people who are pro-life, and pro-choice on the other side. There will be Democrats, and there will be republicans.

Whatever your choices are, is none of my business. That's on you. But stand up for something, if you truly believe that it is what's right.

Now, also look at the evidence and facts on both sides. You have to be objective if you really want to find out the truth.

Action Guide:

1 - Don't be afraid to stand up for something you believe in. However, also look at the facts so you can defend yourself from others' criticism.

2 - Be open to the possibility that you are wrong, or at least, some parts of your beliefs are wrong. That's true humility. Understanding that not everything you believe in is right. Understanding the fact that what you believe now may change overtime. That my friend is real humility.

3 - Stop watching the news. Each side just wants to control their own narrative.

50 - Keep Racking Up Success

Ever seen someone just racking up success after success? Like everything that the personal touch turns to gold?

This is the power of momentum.

Start small, then go big.

That's how everything works.

If you want to be surrounded by great people, if you want to connect with them, and to partner with winners, then you have to be a winner yourself first.

Keep building on that success and keep the momentum going by continuing to take action.

Action Guide:

1 - Notice when you have momentum on your side.

2 - Instead of taking a break and congratulating yourself, focus on achieving more. Go all in and just ride the wave.

Trust me, the momentum will stop. So make sure that you give it a good long ride while it is there.

51 - Take Good Care of Your Physical Health

People will always associate a healthy person to someone whom they can respect.

Why? Because being healthy and appearing healthy gives the impression that you take care of yourself and you care about your well-being.

People like to follow someone aspirational.... If you can do that by being healthy, you'll be able to influence them to follow, admire and respect you.

Action Guide:

1 - Start a healthy habit by walking outside every day for at least 15-20 minutes.

2 - Drink 2 liters of water every day.

52 - Tell Your Truth

They say that the truth will set you free.

It's a cliche, but just like most cliches are, they are true and acceptable.

Telling your truth means being honest with your own feelings and beliefs.

Telling your truth means going for something you believe in, and rejecting the ones that you think aren't serving the world.

When you tell your truth, the right people gravitate towards you and you become someone they can trust.

Action Guide:

1 - Don't be afraid to tell your truth. Don't be someone you are not just so people will like you.

2 - Telling the truth may have some short-term consequences but it will always be the best choice in the long-term.

Conclusion

If there's one thing that I want you to take away from this, is that respect can be earned by being a person of value. And by being a person of value, that means a combination of good character, being good at what you do, being kind, being a leader and a never-ending quest to improve.

Those things get you respect. Those are based on competency. Those are based on things you can control.

These are not tactics, they are long-term strategies for gaining real respect. Respect that is given to someone worth respecting.

So forget about manipulating other people and being a puppet master who relies on fear to get what he wants.

Just be those things that I mentioned above and you will be respected, guaranteed.

Thanks for reading this book and I would really appreciate if you could give this one a quick review on Amazon.

All the best,

A.V. Mendez

I Need Your Help

Hey, did you enjoy this book? Did you found it valuable and actionable? If so, kindly write a short review on Amazon. It would mean a lot to me. Reviews are the lifeblood of every author and the more reviews we get, the more people are likely to discover our work.

Thank you for taking the time to read and good luck in your journey to self-development.

OTHER BOOKS

The 45-Day Self Improvement Handbook: 45 Daily Ideas, Habits and Action-Plan for Becoming More Productive, Persuasive, Influential, Sociable and Self- Confident

Build Confidence & Self-Esteem: 90 Awesome Techniques to Become Confident, Overcome Self-Doubt, Shyness and Improve Your Self-Esteem

How to Focus: 54 Habits, Tools and Ideas to Create Superhuman Focus, Eliminate Distractions, Stop Procrastination and Achieve More With Less Work

Stop Procrastination & Increase Productivity: 60 Tricks on How to Improve Your Focus, Time Management, Habits, Productivity and Overall Ability to Get Things Done

Improving Your Social & People Skills Guidebook: 77 Tricks on How to Improve Your Conversational Skills, Increase Self-Worth, and Become More Confident

Kindly search for "AV MENDEZ" on Amazon to checkout my other books.

www.ingramcontent.com/pod-product-compliance
Ingram Content Group UK Ltd.
Pitfield, Milton Keynes, MK11 3LW, UK
UKHW041642190726
13854UKWH00006B/2654

9 781716 561818